learn to draw
Polar
Animals

**Step-by-step instructions for
25 Arctic & Antarctic wildlife critters**

ILLUSTRATED BY ROBBIN CUDDY

Quarto is the authority on a wide range of topics.
Quarto educates, entertains, and enriches the lives of our readers—
enthusiasts and lovers of hands-on living.
www.quartoknows.com

6 Orchard Road, Suite 100
Lake Forest, CA 92630
quartoknows.com
Visit our blogs @quartoknows.com

MIX
Paper from
responsible sources
FSC® C101537

Printed in China
1 3 5 7 9 10 8 6 4 2

Table of Contents

Tools & Materials

There's more than one way to bring polar animals to life on paper—you can use crayons, markers, colored pencils, or even paints. Just be sure you have plenty of good "polar colors"—blues, purples, grays, and browns.

drawing pencil
and paper

eraser

sharpener

felt-tip markers

colored
pencils

paintbrushes
and paints

How to Use This Book

The drawings in this book are made up of basic shapes, such as circles, triangles, and rectangles. Practice drawing the shapes below.

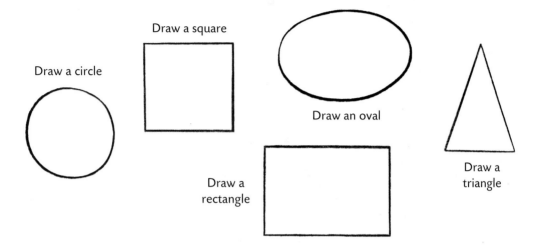

Draw a circle

Draw a square

Draw an oval

Draw a rectangle

Draw a triangle

Notice how these drawings begin with basic shapes.

In this book, you'll learn different facts about each featured polar animal. Look for mini quizzes along the way to see how much you know!

Look for this symbol, and check your answers on page 40!

Adélie Penguin

These adorable birds have a small ring of white feathers around each eye. They also have longer feathers along the tops of their heads that can form small crests.

Mini Quiz

How long do Adélie penguins live?

(Answer on page 40)

Arctic Hare

This hare has a beautiful coat of thick, white fur. Its ears are tipped with black and are shorter than the ears of most hares.

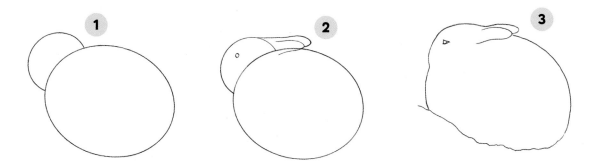

Mini Quiz

How fast can the Arctic hare run?

A. 8 mph

B. 20 mph

C. 40 mph

D. 80 mph

(Answer on page 40)

Blue Whale

Size: 100 feet in length
Weight: 150 tons (300,000 lbs)

Diet: Krill

Location: All oceans, primarily near Antarctica

Blue whales are so large that their hearts alone can weigh around 1,500 pounds!

Fun Fact!

This massive ocean dweller is blue-gray in color with areas of light gray. It has a very small dorsal fin and grooves that run along the underside of its body.

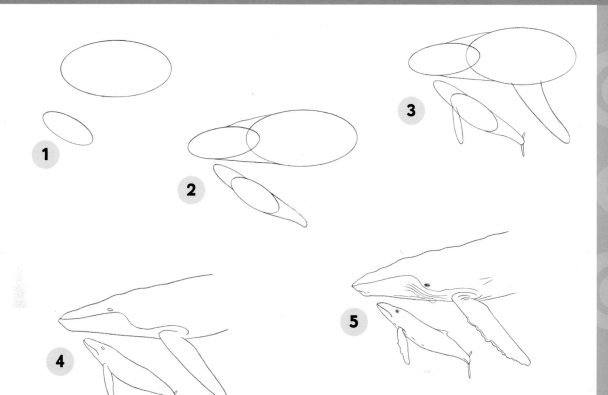

1

2

3

4

5

6

Mini Quiz

True or false: The blue whale is the largest animal that has ever lived on earth.

(Answer on page 40)

Tundra Swan

This elegant, white-feathered bird has a long, curving neck and a black bill, feet, and legs.

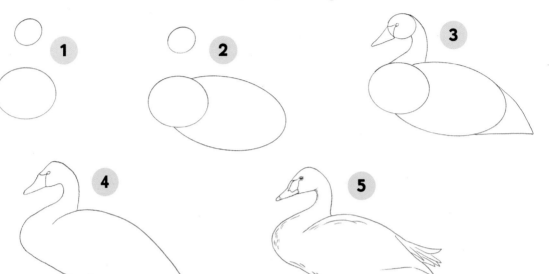

6

Killer Whale

Also called "orcas," these intelligent and distinctly colored mammals are black with white underbellies and patches.

Fun Fact!

Killer whales are actually large dolphins—not whales!

Polar Bear

Location: Arctic island coastlines and ice shelves

Size: 8 feet in length
Weight: 1,600 lbs

Diet: Seals, small walruses, and sometimes small whales

Did You Know?

These powerful, patient hunters have no predators in the wild.

Polar bears have a thick coat of white fur and long hind legs. They also have large, hairy feet and sharp claws that help them walk safely on ice.

Fun Fact!

Polar bears have black skin under their fur to help them absorb warmth from the sun.

Elephant Seal

Size: 21 feet in length
Weight: 4 tons (8,000 lbs)

Diet: Fish and squid

Did You Know?

The elephant seal's color ranges from yellow-brown to blue-gray.

Location: Coasts of California and Baja California; subantarctic regions

This large, loud seal is named for the male's trunk-like snout, which can inflate to produce a "warning" noise for other males.

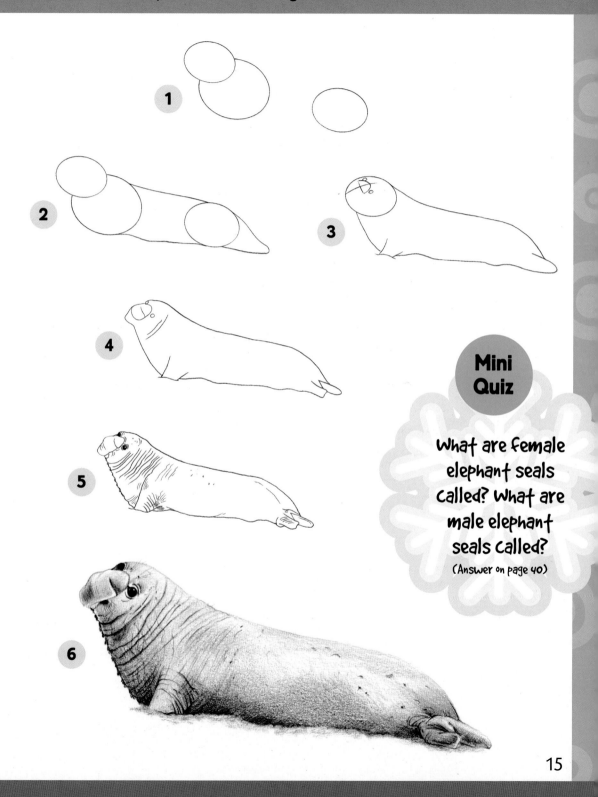

1

2

3

4

5

6

Mini Quiz

What are female elephant seals called? What are male elephant seals called?

(Answer on page 40)

Arctic Tern

The Arctic tern has a rounded head with a black-cap marking.
Its tail has a deep fork, and its beak, legs, and feet are bright red.

Did You Know?

The Arctic tern's gray wings have a span of roughly 33 inches.

Canada Lynx

This exotic-looking wildcat has a grayish-brown coat, a short tail, a facial ruff, and ears tipped with black tufts of hair.

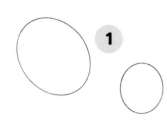

1

2

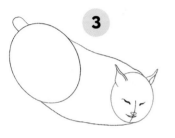

3

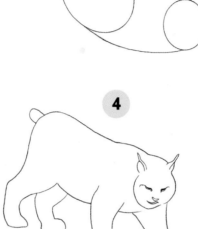

4

Mini Quiz

True or false: The canada lynx is active during the day.

(Answer on page 40)

5

6

Beluga Whale

Details

Size: 15 feet in length
Weight: 3,000 lbs
Location: Coast of the Arctic Ocean
Diet: Fish, crab, squid

Did You Know?

Belugas have 34 teeth for capturing prey: nine pairs on the top and eight pairs on the bottom.

The beluga whale is a beautiful white mammal that lacks a dorsal fin. It has a distinct bulbous forehead, along with a flexible head and neck.

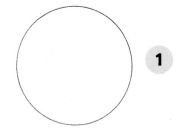

1

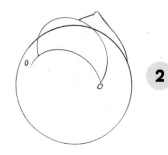

2

3

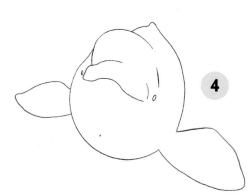

4

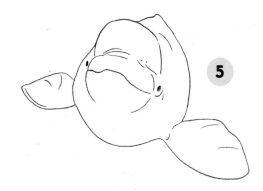

5

6

Mini Quiz

True or false: The beluga whale is found only in the ocean.

(Answer on page 40)

Macaroni Penguin

Size: 20–28 inches in length
Weight: 12 lbs

Location: Rocky coasts and islands of Antarctica, plus islands in the southern Indian and Atlantic oceans

Did You Know?

There are more Macaroni penguins on earth than any other species of penguin.

Diet: Krill, crustaceans, squid, and small fish

This penguin has a distinct yellow-orange crown of feathers on its head. It also has a red bill, red eyes, and a black face.

Fun Fact!

British explorers named the Macaroni penguin because its yellow feathers reminded them of a stylish hat worn in the 18th century, called a "macaroni."

Caribou

Also called "reindeer," caribou are deer with long legs and impressive antlers. A male caribou's antlers can reach 5 feet in length and have up to 40 points!

(Answer on page 40)

Mini Quiz

True or false: Both male and female caribou have antlers.

Puffin

Sometimes called a "sea parrot," this diving bird has a tall, triangular beak and black-and-white markings. Puffins spend the majority of their lives at sea.

Mini Quiz

Where are most of the world's puffins found?

A. Northeastern coast of North America

B. Iceland

C. Northeastern coast of Canada

D. Northern Asia

(Answer on page 40)

Walrus

Details

Size: Up to 12 feet in length
Weight: About 1.5 tons (3,000 lbs)
Location: Arctic Ocean
Diet: Shellfish, fish, and sometimes small seals

Did You Know?

The walrus uses its stiff and sensitive whiskers to find food along the ocean floor.

The walrus is a large, blubbery animal with a small head, whiskers, large tusks, and flat front flippers. These social animals often live in large groups.

1
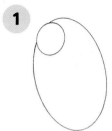

2
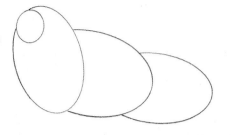

3
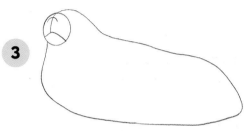

4

5

6

Mini Quiz

What is the purpose of a walrus's tusks?

A. To defend itself
B. To help pull its body from the water onto ice
C. To poke breathing holes into ice
D. All of the above

(Answer on page 40)

Emperor Penguin

Emperor penguins have sleek, regal black-and-white coloring, with yellow and orange accents on their necks and chests.

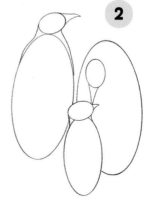 **1**

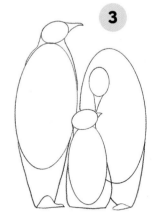 **2**

3

 **4**

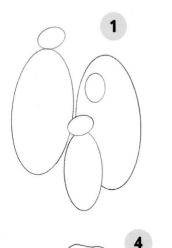 **5**

6

Did You Know?

These penguins can hold their breath underwater for more than 20 minutes.

Ermine

This adorable weasel has a long body, short legs, and a black-tipped tail. To blend in with the snow, its coat turns from mostly brown to white during the winter.

Mini Quiz

True or false: Male and female ermines are the same size.

(Answer on page 40)

Arctic Wolf

Size: Up to 6 feet in length
Weight: 75–125 lbs

Diet: Large herbivores (such as musk-oxen and caribou), small game, seals, and birds

Location: North America and Greenland

Did You Know?

The Arctic wolf is known for its big, sharp teeth; strong jaws; and impressive endurance. They can consume up to 20 pounds of meat in one meal!

The Arctic wolf has a short muzzle, small ears, and a thick, double-coat of white fur that keeps it dry and warm in subzero Arctic temperatures.

Mini Quiz

What is the term for a group of Arctic wolves that hunt and travel together?
A. Pack
B. Pod
C. Herd
D. Kennel
(Answer on page 40)

1

2

3

4

5

6

7

Dall Sheep

These thinhorn sheep have beautiful white coats, yellow eyes, and amber horns. Their hooves have two flexible toes that help them walk on rocky terrain.

1

2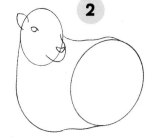

3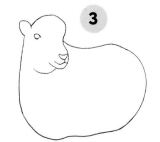

4

5

6

Mini Quiz

What are some differences between male and female Dall sheep?

(Answer on page 40)

30

Harp Seal

Adult harp seals are gray with black markings on their backs that resemble harps or saddles.

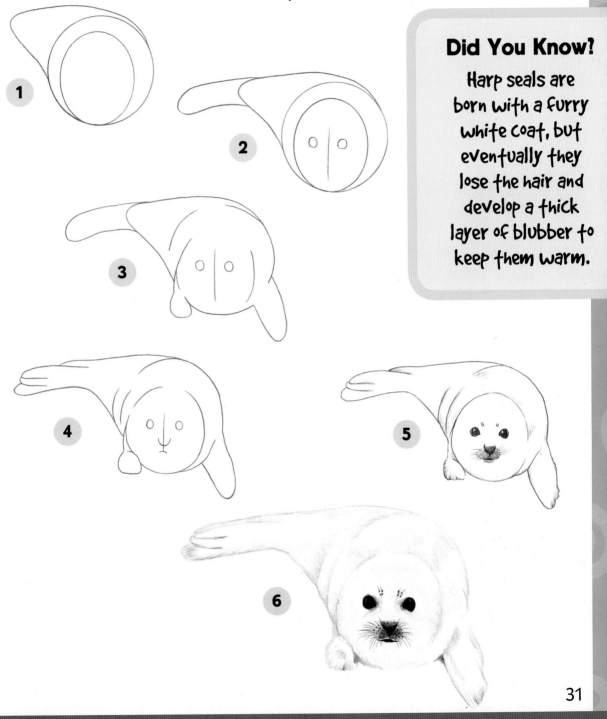

Did You Know?

Harp seals are born with a furry white coat, but eventually they lose the hair and develop a thick layer of blubber to keep them warm.

Humpback Whale

Details

Size: 52 feet in length
Weight: 40 tons (80,000 lbs)
Location: All oceans, from the polar regions to the tropics
Diet: Krill, plankton, and fish

Did You Know?

These musical animals communicate with each other using complex "songs." They also use sounds to hunt and navigate.

The humpback whale has large tail flukes and tubercles (whisker-like bumps) around the mouth. It is often seen breaching or leaping from the water!

Musk-Ox

These cold-weather beasts have long, shaggy brown hair; horns that curve down and out from the face; and hooves that help them walk in the snow.

1

2

3

4

5

6

Fun Fact!

The musk-ox's coat is made up of an outer layer of coarse "guard hairs" and an undercoat of "qiviut" (short, insulating hair). The coat protects them from the cold temperatures of the Arctic.

7

Sled Dog

With thick coats to protect them from frigid temperatures, sled dogs are fast, hardy canines that work in teams to pull sleds through snow and over ice.

Mini Quiz

Which of the following breeds is NOT considered a sled dog:
A. Alaskan Malamute
B. Golden Retriever
C. Eskimo Dog
D. Samoyed
(Answer on page 40)

Narwhal

Details

Size: 17 feet in length
Weight: Up to 3,500 lbs
Location: Arctic coasts and rivers
Diet: Fish, squid, and shrimp

Did You Know?

Only three species of whale live in Arctic waters year-round, including narwhal, beluga, and bowhead whales.

The narwhal is a spotted gray whale with flippers that turn up at the tips. Male narwhals have one long tusk that grows straight out from the upper jaw.

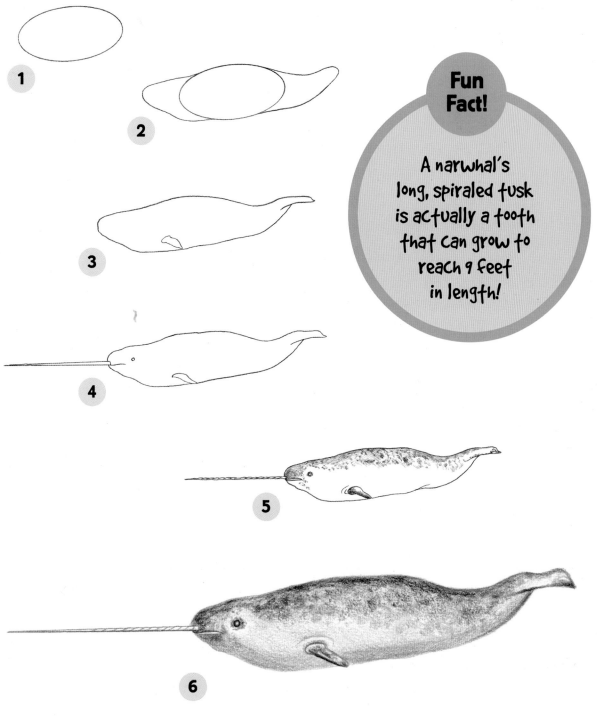

1

2

3

Fun Fact!

A narwhal's long, spiraled tusk is actually a tooth that can grow to reach 9 feet in length!

4

5

6

Arctic Fox

Arctic foxes have beautiful, thick coats of fur and full, bushy tails. Their coats range from blue-gray to brown and white, changing with the seasons.

Fun Fact!

Also known as "polar foxes" or "white foxes," Arctic foxes have fur on the soles of their feet to protect them from the snowy, icy ground of the tundra.

Snowy Owl

The snowy owl has piercing yellow eyes and white feathers that blend into snow. Males are often white, but youngsters and females have dark markings.

Mini Quiz

True or false: The snowy owl is nocturnal, which means that it is most active at night.

(Answer on page 40)

Mini Quiz Answers

Page 6: Adélie penguins can live as long as **20 years.**

Page 7: C. The swift Arctic hare can run as fast as 40 miles per hour.

Page 9: True. The blue whale is even larger than any dinosaur that ever existed.

Page 15: Female elephant seals are called "cows," whereas males are called "bulls."

Page 17: False. The Canada lynx is one of the most elusive wild animals. They are active at night and avoid contact with humans, making them a challenge to spot.

Page 19: False. Beluga whales can be found in rivers, as they feed on salmon returning to sea.

Page 22: True. Caribou are the only deer in which females can have antlers too!

Page 23: B. About 60 percent of the world's puffins are found in Iceland.

Page 25: D. All of the above! A walrus's tusks have many uses.

Page 27: False. Female ermines are much smaller and can be about half the size of male ermines.

Page 29: A. A group of Arctic wolves is called a "pack."

Page 30: Female Dall sheep (called "ewes") are smaller than males (called "rams"). Females also have small, slender horns compared to the large, curling horns of the male.

Page 35: B. Alaskan Malamutes, Eskimo Dogs, and Samoyeds are considered sled dogs, along with others such as Siberian Huskies and Chinooks.

Page 39: False. Unlike most owls, snowy owls hunt during the day.